Taking Shape

From COTTON to T-SHIRT

NICOLA BAXTER

SIMON & SCHUSTER
YOUNG BOOKS

Acknowledgements

The author and publishers would like to thank Cotton Technology International for their assistance.

First published in 1992
by Simon & Schuster Young Books

Simon & Schuster Young Books
Simon & Schuster Ltd
Campus 400, Maylands Avenue,
Hemel Hempstead, Herts HP2 7EZ.

Text and illustrations
© 1992 Simon & Schuster Young Books

Design: Janet Watson
Illustrator: Katy Sleight
Commissioning editor: Debbie Fox

All rights reserved.

Printed in Portugal by Edições ASA
Proost International Book Company.

A CIP catalogue record for this book is available from the British Library.

ISBN 0 7500 1070 3

Contents

All kinds of cotton	8
Growing cotton	10
From fibre to thread	12
From thread to fabric	14
Colouring and finishing	16
From fabric to T-shirt	18
Looking at cotton	20
Make your own fabric	22
Do-it-yourself design	24
Cotton past and present	26
Glossary	28
Index	29

All kinds of cotton

When we think of cotton, it is usually cloth and thread that come to mind. Fibres from the cotton plant can be made into many woven materials, called textiles. But cotton plants can be used to make many other things – even food! Everything here is made partly from the cotton plant.

Which things do you think are made from cotton fibres? Which are made from other parts of the cotton plant?

To understand why the cotton plant is so useful, we need to know more about how it is grown and harvested.

Growing cotton

Cotton plants are grown in warm parts of the world, but they also need plenty of water. The cotton is ready to be picked six or seven months after the seed is planted. In some places cotton is grown in small fields and picked by hand. In other areas machines do most of the work.

Pesticides are sprayed on to the cotton crop to control the insects and diseases that attack it.

Before picking, the cotton may be sprayed with a chemical to make the leaves fall off. This means that less "trash" – leaves and stalks – is picked by the machine.

Flowers appear about two months after the cotton is planted. They last for only three days.

When the flowers die, they leave seed pods, called bolls. Inside are about thirty seeds.

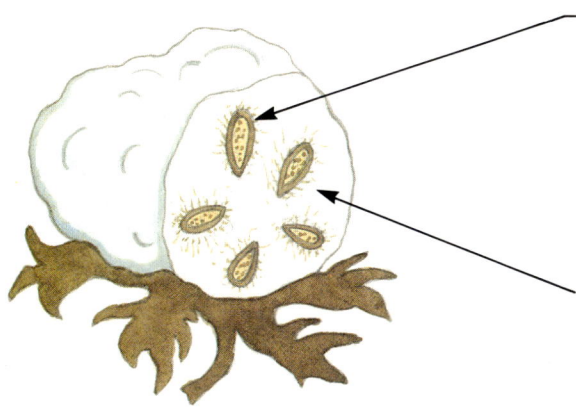

The seeds are covered with tiny fibres called linters. The cellulose in these may be used to make plastics, camera film, explosives and even paper for banknotes.

The fibres, called lint, are made of cellulose. They are used to make thread and woven into textiles.

Tiny fibres start to grow from the seeds. These grow longer and thicker until the boll bursts open and the cotton fibres dry in the sun.

A machine called a gin separates the picked cotton fibres from their seeds. After ginning, the lint is pressed into bales. It is then ready to go to a cotton mill to be made into a textile.

The cotton seeds are not wasted. Cooking oils, soap and cattle feed are made from them.

From fibre to thread

Nowadays making the raw cotton into thread, or yarn, is done by machine. The bales of cotton are opened by machines and air is blown through the lint. This fluffs up the cotton and removes most of the trash that has been left in the bales.

Forming lap

As the trash is removed, the lint is formed into lap, a loose layer of fibres rather like cotton wool from a roll.

Carding into slivers

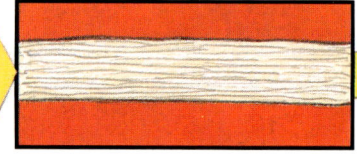

The carding machine combs the lap so that the fibres lie side by side and form a loose rope, called a sliver.

Drawing into roving

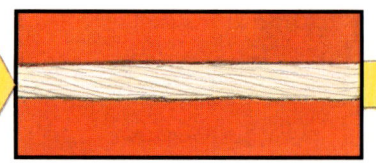

Several slivers are fed into a machine that gently pulls, or draws, them into one thinner sliver, called roving.

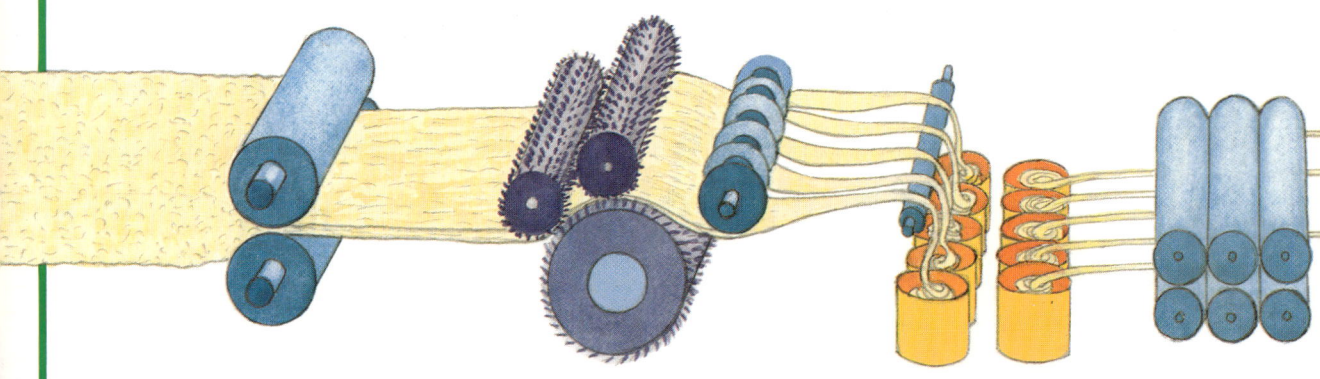

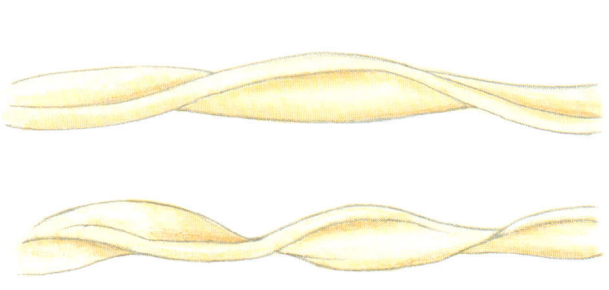

Cotton fibres are 20mm to 50mm long. Under a microscope, the fibres look like a twisted ribbon. This means that the cotton fibres lock strongly together when they are made into thread.

Spinning into yarn

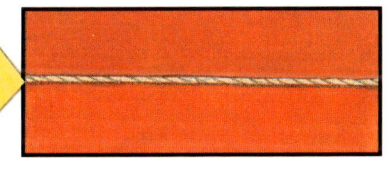

The spinning machine pulls and twists the roving into yarn. First the cotton may be combed to make it stronger and smoother.

 **Try this!**

Yarn can be spun into different thicknesses. It may be thick enough for a knitted jumper or so fine that you can see through a fabric made from it.

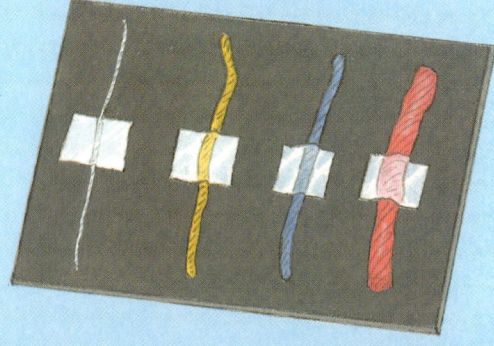

Collect some yarns and try to put them in order of thickness.

From thread to fabric

To make yarn into fabric, it must be either woven or knitted. Weaving and knitting produce fabrics with different properties. Usually woven fabric is firm while knitted fabric is more stretchy.

Woven cloth is made by weaving crossways threads up and down between lengthwise threads.

Knitted cloth is made from one thread formed into loops that link together.

Knitting machines have hundreds of needles holding loops. Some of them produce a tube of fabric rather like the one you can make opposite – but much bigger!

The loops in knitted fabric mean that it can be stretched. It is useful for clothes that need to fit quite tightly.

Even if clothes are made from woven fabric, the wrist and neck openings of clothes are often made of stretchy, knitted fabric. Both woven and knitted fabrics may be found in lots of different patterns.

Try this!

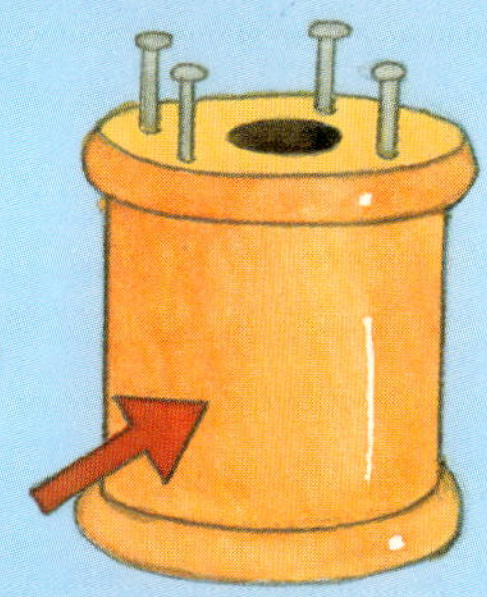

1 Knock four small nails into the top of a wooden cotton reel. You could paint it a bright colour.

2 Push one end of some yarn through the hole in the cotton reel.

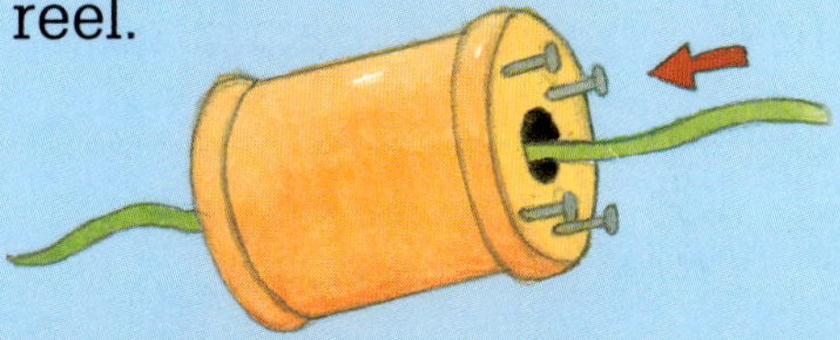

3 Wind the free yarn round the nails as in the picture.

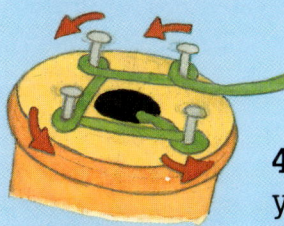

4 Hold the free yarn across the next nail above the loop and use a cocktail stick to lift the loop over the yarn. Then just keep going round!

Soon a knitted tube will start to appear at the bottom.

15

Colouring and finishing

The yellowish colour of raw cotton and the small amounts of a waxy substance left in are not usually wanted in cotton fabric. Machines and chemicals are used to improve the look and feel of the fabric.

The fabric is boiled in a strong chemical to remove the wax. This makes it able to absorb dye. If the cloth is to be white or a pale colour, it is bleached to remove the yellowish colour.

Modern chemical dyes give bright, strong colours that will not fade in sunlight or washing. But people may like the way that older dyes, such as indigo for denim jeans, fades over time.

Great care needs to be taken to use the strong chemicals safely.

16

For patterned fabric, printing is used. This may be done on a large roller printing machine or by screen printing, where dye is squeezed through a mesh on to the fabric beneath. This may be repeated with other colours.

Screen printing may be done on fabric or straight on to a T-shirt!

Often only two colours can give a very attractive pattern.

Fabric can also be treated with chemicals to make it waterproof, flameproof or even creaseproof. It is checked for flaws in the fabric and may be washed and pressed before leaving the factory.

From fabric to T-shirt

Even to make a simple garment like a T-shirt involves many different stages. In a factory, hundreds of T-shirts are made at the same time.

After a designer has decided what the garment will look like, a pattern cutter works out the shape that each piece of fabric needs to be. A T-shirt may need five pieces. The pattern pieces are made in all the different sizes needed.

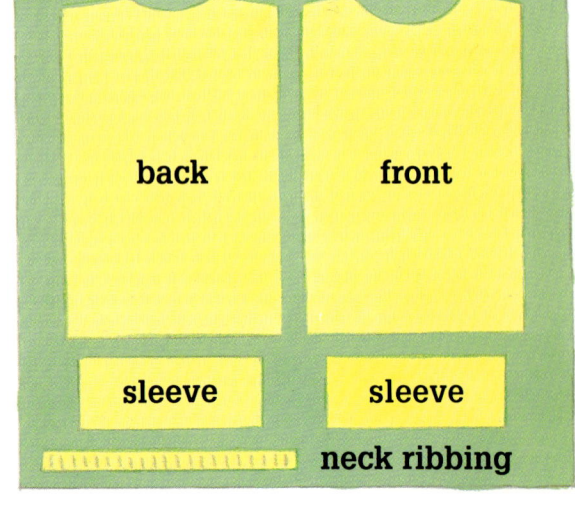

Many layers of material can be cut out at one time, using a band knife. The cutter wears a metal glove for protection.

A lay planner uses a computer to work out the most economical way to fit the pattern pieces on the fabric.

To sew the pattern pieces together, an overlocking sewing machines is used. This has more than one needle, so that the pieces can be joined together and the edges neatened at the same time. This makes sure that the cut edges don't fray.

Labels showing the name of the maker or shop, the size of the garment and how to wash it are sewn in. Then the garment is carefully checked, washed and pressed.

With careful lay planning, not much fabric is wasted. The small pieces that are left can be recycled to make cleaning rags or used to make strong paper for banknotes and documents.

Looking at cotton

You could make a scrapbook of different kinds of fabrics and try these tests to find out more about their properties.
What special properties does cotton have?

Thread patterns

Look carefully at all kinds of cloth and collect small pieces that have interesting woven patterns. Paste them on to card and draw a larger diagram of the weave on squared paper to paste next to the piece of cloth. Can you find out what the different patterns are called?

Stretch test

You will need:

an old T-shirt   scissors
a felt-tip pen   a ruler

1 Measure out a square with sides of 10 cm on the T-shirt and carefully cut it out. Be careful not to stretch the fabric when you measure it.

2 Holding one corner of the square next to the ruler, stretch it as far as you can down the ruler. Measure how far you can stretch it.

3 Now turn the square and measure how much it will stretch the other way. Is there a difference? What happens if you use a piece of woven fabric of the same size?

Absorbency

This means how much liquid the fabric can soak up. Towels need to be able to soak up plenty of water, while sports clothes need to absorb sweat. Waterproof clothes must *not* absorb water!

You will need:

water   a tablespoon
pieces of different fabrics

1 On a safe surface, place a tablespoon of water as though you had spilled it.

2 Use one piece of fabric to wipe up the spill. Make a note of how successful it was.

3 Make a spill for each fabric in turn. Is it just what the fabric is made of that makes a difference, or is it partly the way that it is knitted or woven?

Insulation

This is the way that fabric keeps heat in. Warm clothes for winter need to be good insulators.

You will need:

3 large yoghurt pots with lids
fabric   hot water   elastic bands

1 Wrap different fabrics round two of the pots and fix them with elastic bands. Make sure that they both have the same number of layers of fabric around them.

2 Fill all the pots with hot tap-water and put the lids on.

3 Wait fifteen minutes and then feel or measure how hot the water is. The fabric that is the best insulator will keep the water hottest.

21

Make your own fabric

You can make knitted fabric yourself. You will find it easier to follow these instructions if someone who can knit helps you.

Casting on

Follow the steps below to cast on as many stitches as you need across your knitting.

1 Make a loop like this.

2 Hold the needle in your left hand. Pull the loop tight.

3 Push the other needle through the loop. Bring the yarn between the needles towards you.

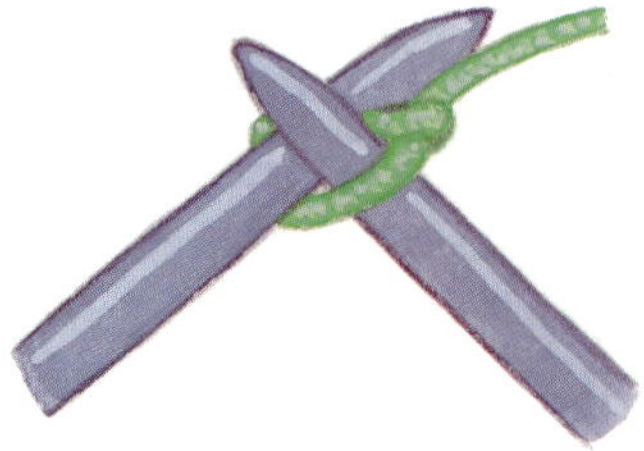

4 Pull the yarn through the first loop to make a new loop.

5 Put the new loop on the lefthand needle next to the first one.

6 Keep doing steps 3, 4 and 5 until you have as many stitches as you need. Putting the needle behind the loop as shown here gives a firmer edging.

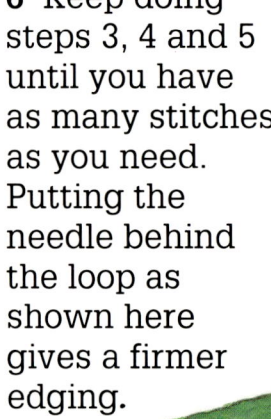 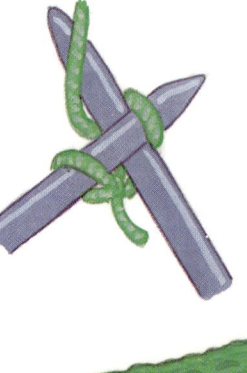

Plain knitting

1 Keeping the needle with the stitches on it in your left hand, push the other needle through the first stitch.

2 Bring the yarn towards you between the needles.

3 With the righthand needle, pull the yarn through in a loop.

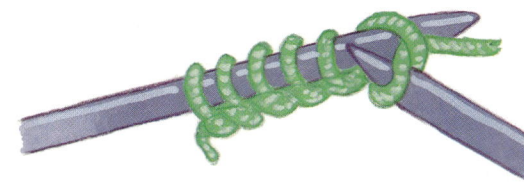

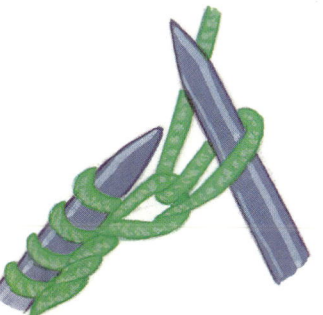

4 Keeping this new loop on your righthand needle, slip the first loop off the other needle and let it drop.

5 Repeat steps 1 to 4 until there are no more stitches. Then change hands for the next row.

Casting off

1 Knit two stitches as before.

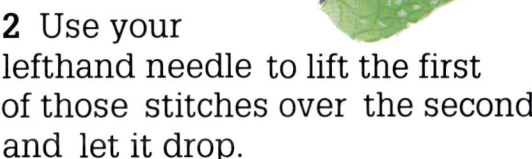

2 Use your lefthand needle to lift the first of those stitches over the second and let it drop.

3 Knit another stitch and again lift the stitch before over it and let it drop.

4 Do the same until you only have one stitch on the righthand needle. Cut your yarn and pull it through the stitch to finish off.

Watch out!

- Don't pull the yarn too tight as you are knitting. It is better for it to be rather loose when you first start.
- Don't worry if your first try is rather funny looking! You'll soon find it easier.

Make a blanket

You could ask all your friends to make knitted squares. When you have enough you could sew them together to make a blanket.

Do-it-yourself design

The design of your T-shirt can tell people what you like or what you believe in – or it can just be fun! You can buy special crayons or paints to use or follow some of the ideas here.

Tie-dye

It is easy to dye a T-shirt in a plain colour by following the instructions on the packet. To add a pattern, you need to find a way of *not* dyeing some parts. Ask an adult to help you.

You will need:

a white T-shirt, washed and ironed
newspaper   an apron
rubber gloves   string
small, clean stones

1 Tie the stones into the T-shirt as in the picture. You can put them on one part of the T-shirt or all over.

2 Ask an adult to help you dye the T-shirt following the instructions on the packet.

3 Rinse, wash and dry your T-shirt. If you like, you can now tie the T-shirt in different ways and dye it again using a different colour. What happens when two dye colours overlap?

Batik

You will need the same things as for tie-dyeing except the string and stones plus:

batik wax   paintbrushes
sticky tape   greaseproof paper

1 Put plenty of newspaper and greaseproof paper inside your T-shirt and tape it down flat on a table.

2 Ask an adult to melt the wax. Then carefully paint it on to the parts of the T-shirt that you do not want to dye.

3 Ask an adult to help you dye the T-shirt, dry it and remove the wax by ironing between sheets of newspaper.

4 You can dye the T-shirt again using another colour and putting the wax in different places.

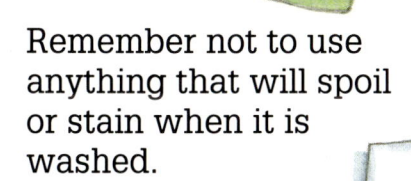

Design additions

With some simple sewing, you can decorate your T-shirts by adding buttons, beads, braid, ribbon, cotton yarn and coloured cloth.

Remember not to use anything that will spoil or stain when it is washed.

Cotton past . . .

- Traces of cotton fabrics have been found in Mexico dating back nearly 7,000 years.

- The word "cotton" comes from Arabic "qutun". It was brought to Europe when the Moors conquered Spain over a thousand years ago.

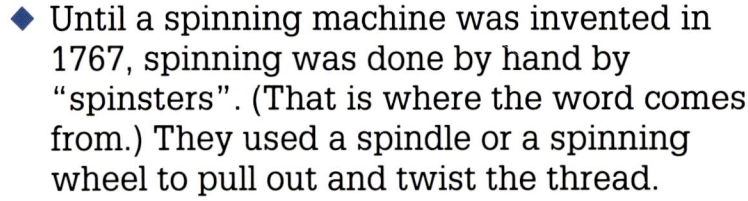

- Before chemical bleaches were discovered, all fabric was laid out in the sun to fade. It might take months!

- Until a spinning machine was invented in 1767, spinning was done by hand by "spinsters". (That is where the word comes from.) They used a spindle or a spinning wheel to pull out and twist the thread.

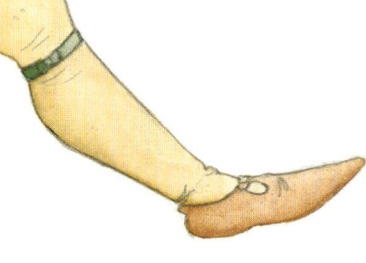

- The first knitting machine was invented by William Lee in the 1580s. Knitted fabric had become very popular because it was stretchy and good for stockings. In those days men liked to show off their legs!

. . . and present

◆ T-shirts were first worn as underwear by men in the last century. Later they were worn by American soldiers. It wasn't until the 1970s that they really became popular as everyday clothes for everyone.

◆ Half of the textile fibre used in the world every year is cotton.

◆ Because so much cotton is now picked by machine, scientists have developed plants where all the bolls are ready for picking at the same time.

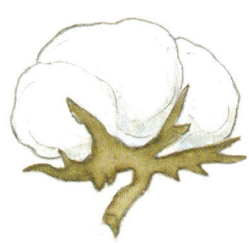

◆ The amount of land used to grow cotton is about the same today as it was in 1930. Advances in plant breeding and farming mean that this land now produces nearly three times as much cotton as in 1930.

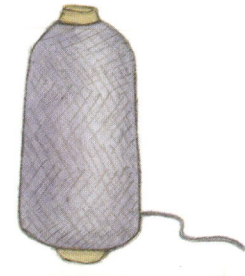

◆ A modern spinning machine can spin 250 metres of thread in one minute.

Glossary

Absorbency
This describes how much liquid a fabric can soak up.

Bleach
A chemical that can remove colour from yarn or fabric.

Boll
The seed pod of the cotton plant, in which the cotton fibres grow.

Carding
Combing cotton fibres so that they lie straight and side by side.

Cellulose
A substance within plants.

Cotton
A plant producing fine hair-like fibres, or the yarn or fabric made from them.

Fabric
Cloth made from fibres.

Finishing
Preparing fabric by washing, pressing and treating.

Gin
A machine that separates cotton fibres from cotton seeds.

Insulation
How well heat is kept in.

Knitting
Making fabric by looping threads together.

Lap
Cotton fibres formed into a loose layer like a roll of cotton wool.

Lint
The longer fibres that grow inside a cotton seed pod.

Pesticide
A chemical to kill insects and diseases that attack plants.

Roving
A loose rope of cotton fibres, thinner than a sliver.

Screen printing
Printing a pattern or picture on fabric by squeezing dye through a mesh screen on to the fabric. One colour is applied at a time.

Spinning
Making yarn from fibres by pulling and twisting them together.

Textile
Fabric made by weaving or knitting.

Trash
Leaves, stalks and dirt that have to be removed from cotton fibres.

Weaving
Making fabric by passing threads over and under each other to form a mesh.

Yarn
Thread made by stretching and twisting fibres together.

Index

absorbency 21

batik 25
bleaching 16, 26, 28

carding 12, 28
cellulose 11, 28
chemicals 10, 16, 26
cloth 8, 14, 15, 20, 25
clothes 15, 17, 18, 21, 26
colouring 16, 17, 24, 25
combing 12, 13
computer 18
cotton bolls 10, 11, 27, 28
cotton mill 11
cotton picking 10, 11, 27
cotton plants 8, 9, 10, 27
cotton, raw 11, 12, 16
cotton seed 10, 11
creaseproofing 17
cutting 18

designing 18, 24, 25
dyeing 16, 17, 24, 25, 28

fabric 8, 13, 14, 16, 17, 18, 19, 20, 21, 22, 23, 26, 28

fibre 8, 11, 12, 13, 27, 28
finishing 16, 17, 28
flameproofing 17
fraying 19

gin 11, 28
ginning 11
growing 10, 11, 27

indigo 16
insulation 21, 28

knitted fabric 14, 15, 22, 23, 26, 28
knitting machine 15, 26

labelling 19
lap 12, 28
lay planning 18, 19
lint 11, 12, 28
linter 11, 28

paper 11, 19
pattern 15, 17, 18, 20, 24, 25
pattern cutting 18
pesticide 10, 28
pressing 17, 19
printing 17

properties 14, 20

recycling 11, 19
roving 12, 28

screen printing 17, 28
sewing 19, 25
size 18, 19
sliver 12, 28
spinning 13, 26, 27, 28
stretchiness 14, 15, 20
sunlight 16, 26

textile 8, 11, 13, 27, 28
thread 8, 11, 12, 13, 14, 20, 26
tie-dyeing 24, 25
trash 10, 12, 28
T-shirt 17, 18, 20, 24, 25, 27

washing 16, 17, 19
waste 19
waterproofing 17, 21
weaving 14, 15, 20

yarn 12, 13, 14, 15, 22, 23, 25

29